ETHICAL LIVING™

ETHICAL
PET OWNERSHIP

LUCY K. SHAW

Rosen
YA™

New York

Published in 2020 by The Rosen Publishing Group, Inc.
29 East 21st Street, New York, NY 10010

First Edition

Library of Congress Cataloging-in-Publication Data

Names: Shaw, Lucy K., 1987– author.
Title: Ethical pet ownership / Lucy K. Shaw.
Description: First edition. | New York : Rosen Publishing, 2020
| Series: Ethical living | Audience: Grade 7–12. | Includes bibliographical references and index.
Identifiers: LCCN 2017055273| ISBN 9781508180616 (library bound) | ISBN 9781508180623 (paperback)
Subjects: LCSH: Pet owners—Juvenile literature.
Classification: LCC SF411.4 .S53 2019 | DDC 636.088/7—dc23
LC record available at https://lccn.loc.gov/2017055273

Manufactured in the United States of America

CONTENTS

INTRODUCTION 4

CHAPTER ONE
IS HAVING A PET ETHICAL? 7

CHAPTER TWO
WHICH TYPE OF ANIMAL CAN YOU LOVE BEST?...................16

CHAPTER THREE
ADOPTING YOUR PET 25

CHAPTER FOUR
BRINGING YOUR NEW ANIMAL COMPANION HOME 34

CHAPTER FIVE
DAILY LIFE TOGETHER 43

GLOSSARY 53
FOR MORE INFORMATION 55
FOR FURTHER READING 58
BIBLIOGRAPHY......................................59
INDEX 62

INTRODUCTION

Having a pet brings companionship and profound happiness to millions of people all over the world. And for an animal, being a pet can provide many animals with a loving home and an apparently happy life. We like to think that our pets love us as much as we love them, and often it really feels like that is true. We think of them as part of the family. But this culture of keeping animals in our homes, often for our own whims and pleasure, also raises some important moral questions. Even when we love our pets and even when we do treat them like smaller, furrier members of the family, there is this nagging feeling that it must be, in some way, a selfish act to take a living creature and say it belongs to us. It's not as though it has any way to consent.

On our quest toward living ethically, we must start by questioning day-to-day societal norms and acting on the weak spots we uncover as we go. The world of animal companionship is complex; we need to ask whether it can ever be ethical to actually own another living animal—as well as ponder, why do we even want to?

As we closely examine our good intentions, we will discover that, traditionally, many now-obvious ways in

We often consider animal rights in relation to eating meat, wearing fur, or animal testing by cosmetics companies. Being more conscious of animals' best interests can also start at home.

which we can better care for our animals have been overlooked. And we will start to understand why that has been the case. We will place ourselves close to the beginning of the journey toward animal rights, while educating ourselves on the history of animal domestication, and all the while anticipating and preparing for a glorious future in which all animals will ascend beyond the legal status of a piece of property. We will consider the theoretical side of these ideas, while focusing on the practical steps we can take toward ethical pet ownership. Because the truth is that we, as a species, love bonding with our pets. There is something truly unique about the friendships we can have with the individual animals we come to love. There is something deeply profound about an interspecies pack of humans and animals living together in harmony under one roof. We just might need to update some of our ideas about taking care of animals and bring them in line with our twenty-first century values.

Contemplating these issues is just as important for people who are considering adopting their first pet as it is for those who have already kept their companion animal for some time. There is always more we can learn about our pets, and always more we can learn from them, if we truly take the time to observe and listen. The relationship between a person and a pet should be a reciprocal bond, and we can rest assured our pets will always do their part. It's up to us to do our research and to always put our pets' best interests first, just as we would for any family member.

Chapter One

IS HAVING A PET ETHICAL?

We may take it for granted and accept it as completely natural, but it is important to remember that the domestic relationships we have with other species have evolved over thousands of years to reach the point at which we find ourselves now. While we often come to love our pets as we do our siblings or parents and to think of them as an extra, fluffier member of the family, we must also educate ourselves on the particularities of their needs and continually try to question whether we are giving them the kind of life they deserve. To do this, we first need to understand how pets came into our homes and lives, how we came to develop the special relationships we have with certain types of animals, and how we came to need each other in all the different ways we do.

A BRIEF HISTORY OF PETS

Over many thousands of years, animals and humans have coevolved to reach this symbiotic contract: we take care of our pets by providing shelter, food, medical care, and protection from the crueler aspects of a life in the wild, while they in turn provide us with a number of things that we need, too, such as companionship, emotional support, protection from intruders to ours homes, and the exercise we get from taking our pets outside. The list of benefits from owning a pet could be endless. And all good pet owners will tell you that while the early morning winter walks can be grueling, changing the litter box is an unglamorous part of a daily routine, or the price of veterinary care can become overwhelming, pets do bring an inconceivable

The wordless bond between you and your animal companion is a priceless gift. It would be hard to find anyone else so happy to see you walk through the door after a long day.

amount of joy into our lives. We give to them, and we receive unexpected gifts in return.

It is an unspoken contract though, obviously, because animals can never truly communicate if they are happy with the circumstances in which they find themselves. But they can give us some clues, and we really do often experience true and meaningful bonds with our animals. Many dog owners, for example, have experienced the profound sensitivity that their pets can convey in response to times of difficulty or sadness. It is not uncommon for a dog to jump up onto its owner's lap when he or she is feeling upset, as if to say, "It's OK! I'm here! And I'm cute! So don't worry!" Our pets can make us smile when we feel like crying. And so it only seems fair that we remember the great responsibility we have to their emotional needs, as well as their more practical needs, in return. Even if we can't communicate with animals verbally, or perhaps *especially* because we cannot communicate with them using language, we must make a conscious effort to take note of their emotional ups and downs, to try our best to understand what makes them happy and comfortable.

The history of pets is essentially the history of animal domestication, which, by definition, means the permanent genetic modification of a bred lineage that leads to an inherited predisposition toward humans. Or in other words, we as humans have purposefully, biologically influenced the reproduction of certain animals in order to secure a more predictable supply of the resources we wish to obtain from them. Domestication isn't about taming animals we find in the wild over the course of one lifetime, but rather about taming entire species over the course of millennia, molding their temperaments and their physicalities in order to make them better suited to helping us. Humans have traditionally seen animals as a type of property that should provide us with some kind of service. When we bring our own pets into this context, things quickly start to feel complicated!

ANIMALS IN THE HOME

Unsurprisingly perhaps, given the special relationship that we have with them now, the first animals to be domesticated by humans were most likely dogs. Based on paintings and carvings found in ancient campsites and tombs in Mesopotamia, dogs may have been tamed and kept as pets since Paleolithic times. We're talking tens of thousands of years ago. And of course, humans have changed a lot since then, too! The history of animal domestication is intertwined with the history of human domestication. We're all evolving together.

Based on recent DNA comparisons of living species, it is estimated that cats were first domesticated from Middle Eastern wildcats as early as ten thousand years ago. And thousands of years later (still thousands of years ago from today), they became an important part of ancient Egyptian culture, even being worshipped as part of a religion that idolized animals.

Believe it or not, our sweet and fluffy friends are evolutionary master-pieces. It's been a fifty-five million year journey from the miacis, the prehistoric weasel-like ancestor of the dog, to the labradoodle.

We might think we're obsessed with our pets, but the ancient Egyptians literally worshipped their cats. Presumably, the cats loved it.

Cats were celebrated for their ability to hunt vermin and snakes, and they became a symbol of grace and poise within Egyptian culture, but it is still unclear what their emotional relationship with humans was really like at that stage in history.

PETS TODAY

Now that we have all of this information, we need to ask ourselves, is it really ethical for us to bring animals into our homes? Is the love that we think we can give to a pet as natural and as pure as it may feel to us? Is it really what an animal wants or needs? Can we really justify using animals to service our selfish desires? Should we simply let all of our pets free and release them into the wild?

Of course, the answer to this last question is no. We cannot and should not open our doors and windows and set our pets free. The animals we now keep as pets

WHAT ARE PETS FOR?

The primary bond distinguishing the modern relationship between a pet and an owner is affection, but throughout history, this has not been their only function. Traditionally, one of the most fundamental uses of pets has been for catching other animals to feed their human masters. Dogs, cats, and birds have been trained to hunt other animals for humans to eat. Some pets, most typically cats, can be trained to hunt other animals that are considered pests, like mice, rats, and snakes. Many breeds of dog have been developed to specialize in herding other animals, like sheep or cattle.

Sheepdogs can be trained to herd geese. Does that make them geese dogs? The world of animals is complex and fascinating!

(continued on the next page)

(continued from the previous page)

Pets have also been used for the purpose of guarding—a home or territory, humans themselves, or even other animals on a farm. Although dogs are the most common example, any pet with a strong sense of smell or hearing, and with the ability to make a loud noise, can be used as a guard. In ancient Egypt, it is thought that humans kept geese for this purpose!

More recently, domesticated animals themselves have become a consumer product or commodity for humans. Pets are now bred for a plethora of purposes, including aesthetics, show careers, and racing or competitive sports, and their monetary value as breeding animals is part of a self-perpetuating industry.

would not be able to survive in the wild. They have been bred specifically over thousands of years to depend on humans. And therein lies the answer to the question of whether having a pet can be considered ethical. We now have a deep responsibility to care for our animals and to treat them with respect. Fortunately, if we become and stay informed about their needs, we can make a lot of good choices in order to do just that.

Currently, in the United States, while pets enjoy growing social acceptance, the law is playing catch-up. Animal rights activists and legislators are slowly paving the way for legal rights for animals, who currently have the legal status of a piece of property, the same as, say, a couch or a microwave. However, just over the border in Canada, several provinces have passed legislation that better protects animals and defines them, not as pieces of property to be owned, but as sentient beings. This means that the law recognizes a pet's ability to perceive and feel things. You cannot own a sentient being, but you can be its legal guardian. This is an important step in the journey for animal rights.

Human beings have been keeping animals as pets since prehistoric times, and this phenomenon exists in almost every culture. It seems to satisfy a deep-rooted universal human desire. For now, questioning the ethics of pet ownership is a largely theoretical endeavor. The reality is that we, as a species, do have pets, and we, as a species, have a responsibility to take care of them.

Chapter Two

WHICH TYPE OF ANIMAL CAN YOU LOVE BEST?

Choosing which kind of pet you should add to your family is a very important and serious decision and should not be made without very careful consideration. You must consider not only how long your pet is likely to live, but also what kind of changes are likely to happen in your own life during those years. Will you be able to provide stability for your pet over the course of its lifetime if you're heading off to college or moving from your family home and out into the world? Will you be able to afford to care for it and have the time to give it the attention it deserves? And will you be able to leave it in capable hands if you travel? Or travel with it in a way that is comfortable and not distressing for your pet, should you need to?

MAKING SPACE FOR A PET

A huge determining factor in choosing which kind of pet to get is your surrounding environment. Do you have the kind of space required for keeping a healthy animal? Obviously, a large dog demands a bigger home than a hamster. It is necessary to do specific research into the needs of whichever sort of animal you're thinking of bringing home. Often, as a culture, we can have outdated—or just plain inaccurate— ideas about what different animals really need, and some of these myths have been around for centuries. It can be difficult to know where the facts end and where speculation, fictional inventions, or even carefully orchestrated commercial hoaxes begin, so always make sure to do as much research and planning as possible before deciding to bring any kind of animal into your life.

Another thing to keep in mind when choosing your pet is that all animals are extremely sensitive and can be severely harmed by a lack of stimuli in their environ-ment. A pet is more likely to be badly behaved when it's bored, which is obviously negative for everyone in your home, including your pet. But it's not as simple as keeping it busy with treats and toys. You must consider the kind of attention your pet is getting, too.

For example, birds need to be able to fly and to be social with other birds, and it is therefore unethical to keep them in small cages, especially by themselves. Contrary to popular belief, cats thrive on interaction with humans. They may have a reputation for being low-maintenance pets, compared to dogs especially, but they do enjoy being nurtured by their guardians and, what's more, appreciate consistency. A lot of

In the wild, many birds will travel thousands of miles each year as part of their migration to warmer climates. Flying long distances is integral to their nature.

cats like to know exactly what is going to happen and when it's going to happen in order to feel relaxed. Becoming in tune with your pet's needs is something to strive for and something that will take time and effort to achieve.

While some animals are best suited to a quiet life with just one or two people, others can enjoy the playfulness of a house filled with children and other animals. This isn't just about choosing a specific species or breed of pet, but about getting to know the temperament of a particular animal before you make your decision. You will need to consider both the animal's

It can be easy to forget that we're all a part of the same food chain. A cat threatening a bird gives a worm somewhere a moment's peace.

background and how it might be able to fit into your family. Remember, your pet is quickly going to come to rely on you for its mental and physical well-being. You need to think of everything!

THE FOOD CHAIN

Consider the impact that your pet could have on local wildlife, too. Are there native species in the area to which your pet could cause damage? And if so, would it be ethical to put your pet in that position? Both cats and dogs will often hunt birds, lizards, frogs, and mice, if given the opportunity. On the other hand, are there native species in the area with the potential to cause harm to your pet? In heavily forested areas, for

WHAT ABOUT EXOTIC PETS?

The exotic pet trade is a huge multinational industry, and selling protected wildlife is one of the most lucrative sources of criminal activity in the world. Unfortunately, it often ends up being the animals who pay the price for these crimes. Animals are often captured from their native environments, separated from their families, and subjected to grueling transportation around the globe in poor conditions. This is clearly not an ethical practice, and many do not survive. But even when exotic animals are acquired legally, is it fair to keep them in our homes?

Exotic pets can be dangerous to humans, too. Animals pulled from the wild are more likely to spread infectious diseases and more likely to lash out at their guardians, who are not typically well equipped to deal with their needs. While

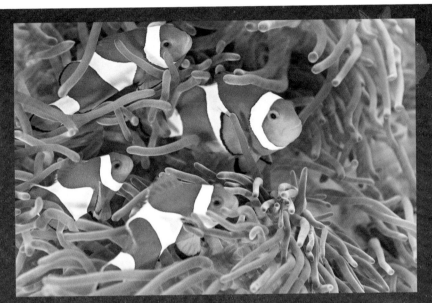

Clownfish kept in captivity have only half the life expectancy of those left in the wild. As they have few ocean predators, humans are actually their biggest threat.

humans have developed relationships with some species over thousands of years, we haven't done the same with others. Simply plucking reptiles or fish from tropical climates and keeping them in tanks is not beneficial to those animals. They do not need to be taken care of by people.

Caring for exotic animals is complicated, and the information readily available to us is often inconsiderate of an animal's needs. For example, reptiles are often branded by pet stores as needing minimal, rather than specialized, care. But every species of reptile requires highly specific conditions and levels of socialization. Owners can rarely provide adequate conditions for them based on the information available. It simply isn't natural for these creatures to be kept in our homes. Respect for wild animals means leaving them in the wild.

example, there could be coyotes or bears. Would it be it safe for your pet to go outside unaccompanied if there are potential predators in the area? It is always important to recognize the presence and value of other animals beyond the ones you know!

MAKING AN INFORMED DECISION

Once you've done your research and weighed all of the information you've gathered, you may decide that you're not ready to take on the responsibility of caring

Offering your time and love to animal shelters is helpful for everyone. A few hours of attention for an animal yet to find a family can have a huge impact on its emotional well-being.

for a pet just yet. And that's OK! There are still plenty of ways you can expand on your love for animals and gain experience for the future. You could volunteer at an organization like the American Society for the Prevention of Cruelty to Animals (ASPCA), the Humane Society, or Defenders of Animal Rights. You could volunteer to pet sit for a friend or family member if he or she is going on vacation. Or accompany a friend when he or she is out walking his or her dog. The more time you spend around other people's animals, the quicker you will start to get a feel for whether you're ready to have your own pet.

One very important thing to remember is that you should only take the plunge and welcome a new family member into your home if you're really sure that you want to take on the responsibility of caring for another living creature. Sure, some days will be magical, and you will have so much fun. The rewards will feel endless. But other days, you might be busy or sick or tired or feeling broke, and you'll still have to put your pet's needs first. Only you can decide when you're ready to become a guardian to a beautiful, sentient being and a new best friend! Once you have learned as much as you can to prepare and decided it's time to meet it, your pet will be lucky to have you.

MYTHS AND FACTS

Myth: Cats need to be allowed to roam free outside.

Fact: Cats are generally healthier and have the potential to live longer when they are kept inside. However, cats can and should be exercised! Games and toys can stimulate them mentally and physically to keep them active and at a healthy weight.

Myth: Rabbits live for only a few years, so getting one isn't a long-term commitment.

Fact: Well-cared-for indoor rabbits often live for seven to ten years, and sometimes even into their teens! This is a similar life span to some breeds of dog and requires the same long-term commitment.

Myth: Dogs that run around all day in the backyard don't need to go for walks.

Fact: Taking your dog for a walk is important because it imitates the way that a dog pack works together, by moving through a territory as part of a group, toward a certain goal. Although a dog may burn off energy by running around in the yard, that kind of energy is unfocused and can lead to anxiety or nervousness in your pet.

Chapter Three

ADOPTING YOUR PET

If you have decided that you're ready to bring a pet into your life, congratulations! This is really exciting news. Assuming that you have already decided which type of animal is best suited to you and your lifestyle, and which type of animal you can give the best life to, the next thing you need to consider is where you're going to find this animal! There are many different ways of acquiring pets, and unsurprisingly, they're not all equal or ethical. Just when you thought you'd finished your research, here comes another step.

DOING THE RIGHT THING

Your first thought might be to go to a local pet store or to contact an animal breeder because it's possible to purchase young and beautiful animals from these places. The animals look so cute in the window! And the chances of these potential pets having preexisting behavioral issues might seem lower than if you were to find them at a shelter. They're only babies, after all. But it is crucial to keep in mind that there is currently an overpopulation crisis of animal companions in America. Every year, over six million dogs and cats enter animal shelters in the United States!

Some of these dogs and cats are lucky enough to be adopted into loving families. But there are far more animals in desperate need of a new home than there are considerate people who want to adopt them. Unfortunately, for every animal who is purchased from a store or breeder, another one loses the chance to be adopted from an animal shelter. It is therefore very important to consider the consequences of supporting an industry that profits from churning out "designer" animals.

A responsible breeder would never sell an animal to a pet store; he or she would want to screen a potential guardian first to ensure that his or her animal is going to a good

You will feel a sense of pride every time someone asks where you got your pet when you can say that you rescued her from a shelter and saved her life!

WHERE DO THE PETS AT PET STORES COME FROM?

Virtually all of the pets found in pet stores are sourced from animal mills. Animal mills are large-scale commercial breeding facilities that prioritize financial profit over the well-being of their animals. These types of breeding operations exist for the mass production of puppies, kittens, rabbits, rodents, and almost every other kind of animal readily available to buy in pet stores today. Mill animals are raised in the mill until they're only a few weeks old, sold to wholesalers or directly to pet stores for very low prices, then marked up by the store to be sold to anyone who has the money to buy them.

It's not that all people who buy animals from pet stores or breeders are cruel or selfish. Many are simply unaware. Animal rights activists are working every day to change this.

(continued on the next page)

(continued from the previous page)

Mills usually house young animals in overcrowded and unsanitary conditions, without adequate veterinary care, food, water, or socialization. Animals are often kept in cages with wire flooring that injures their paws and legs—and it is not unusual for cages to be stacked on top of one another in columns. Females in animal mills are almost constantly pregnant, with little to no recovery time between litters. Once they have been physically exhausted to the point that they can no longer reproduce, breeding females are often killed. The cruel reality is that the mother of a puppy in a pet store window is unlikely to make it out of a mill alive.

Even a baby rabbit who makes it out of a breeding facility and then survives the long truck ride to a pet store is not guaranteed a happy or healthy life. Pet stores that sell live animals are not generally known for careful attention to their "products." In poor and overcrowded conditions, diseases can spread quickly, and many animals die within their first few days at the store. The animals who do prevail spend their time at the store being handled by large numbers of people and most likely being cared for by staff untrained in the specifics of their particular species. In order to be an ethical pet companion, it is imperative to avoid buying animals from pet stores!

home. But even a responsible breeder with the best of intentions for his or her animals is contributing to the overpopulation crisis, not to mention the health problems that can arise from overbreeding or from trying to create "designer" pets. Dachshunds can have chronic back problems; pugs can have difficulty breathing. It is heartbreaking to think of the hidden suffering many animals go through due to our desire as humans to have them look cute.

BE A HERO

Given all of this information, there is simply no good reason for buying a pet from a pet store or a breeder. Rehoming an animal from a shelter is always the best option. Animals in shelters have almost always ended up there through no fault of their own. We can't, in good conscience, leave them there, while supporting the self-perpetuating animal-production industry. Besides, what could be better than the feeling of knowing that you have saved a life?

There are also many benefits to adopting your pet from an animal shelter. For one thing, it's actually much cheaper than buying your pet from a breeder or a pet store. And shelters and rescue groups often include vaccinations, microchipping, and spaying or neutering as part of the adoption fee. What's more, you can trust that you're in the hands of people who have really cared for your pet, rather than people who are simply in it for the money, so the transition process for the animal as it enters your life can be catered toward its particular needs and temperament. You're also freeing up a space at the shelter, so another animal in need can be cared for!

Because they're often older than the animals found in pet stores, a lot of "preowned" animals are already house trained. And because animals in shelters have already gained some life experience, you have a good chance of being able to find an animal that fits

Kittens are so cute that it's hard to resist taking them home, but they should never be separated from their mothers until they're old enough. Usually that is at about twelve weeks old.

appropriately with your lifestyle and personality. You should talk to the volunteers and staff members who know your potential pet personally. They will be invested in finding a good match for both of you.

It is important and fun to research your local animal shelters online before you visit. Not only can you often view detailed descriptions of the animals currently hoping to be rescued, but you can get a feel for the kind of experience the animals are having there and read up on advice from the shelter on how to prepare for welcoming your new animal friend. Once an adoption is in process, it can happen very quickly. You should be sure that you really want to rescue an animal before you visit the shelter. The emotional impact of seeing all of those animals in need can be overwhelming, and sometimes people can make decisions they haven't prepared for. The last thing you want to do is cause an animal more stress by not being able to provide for it long term.

ANIMAL SHELTER EUTHANASIA

Although the number of animals killed in shelters is decreasing every year, there are still healthy animals being put to sleep every day because nobody wants to adopt them. According to the most recent statistics from the National Council on Pet Population Study and Policy, which date back to 1997, around three million animals in US shelters are euthanized every year—that's 56 percent of dogs and 71 percent of cats in the United States. Only around a quarter of animals who enter these facilities are actually adopted by new families.

Reportedly, cats are put down in higher numbers because it is less likely they will have any kind of identification on their bodies when they are taken to the shelter. It is really important for your pet to have some kind of official identification, even if it is always kept indoors. Sadly, a large portion of strays in shelters are indoor animals that escaped from their homes and could not be returned.

BE REALISTIC

If you don't feel ready to commit to adopting a pet for its whole life, you might be interested in fostering one on a short-term basis. This way, you would be able to give an animal a happy temporary home while the local shelter searches for its forever family. Foster care providers play a huge role in a rescue animal's life, and shelters will typically provide you with full support and advice regarding the animal you're caring for, as well as equip you with everything you need to look after it, such as food and bedding.

Nourishing and caring for a new pet requires time, commitment, and a gentleness you may not yet know you possess.

When it comes to adopting your animal companion, no matter where you choose to find it, it's important to use your intuition. Remember, every single animal has its own personality and temperament, just like humans do. Make a conscious effort to bond with your pet before you bring it home, and you are much more likely to have a happy life together. The short time you spend at the shelter is going to have a huge impact on the rest of your life! You just gained a new family member.

Chapter Four

BRINGING YOUR NEW ANIMAL COMPANION HOME

Preparing your home for your new animal companion is a fun and exciting process to be enjoyed and savored in anticipation of the arrival of your new friend. Exactly what and how much you will need to do will depend on the kind of pet you have chosen. For some pets, you will need to buy more specialized equipment, while for others you will need to make simple changes toward animal proofing your existing layout, like moving electrical cords out of sight and moving plants out of reach. If you are adopting from a shelter, the staff there should be able to provide you with a checklist of things you can do to make sure you're fully prepared before your animal friend arrives. And it never hurts to do your own research, too! In fact, as we continue to learn, research is a major part of your preparation at every step of this journey. Thinking of more ways to make your pet comfortable is a never-ending part of your relationship.

But while this is sure to be an exciting time, it could also be a stressful time for both you and your

Just as you might love the feeling of fresh sheets on your bed, your pet likes to have a clean, warm place to sleep, too.

new animal companion. It is easy to underestimate how much time it might take to introduce your new arrival to its new home and family and how much time it might take for it to feel completely comfortable with you, which is understandable. Imagine how you have felt going into new environments by yourself and meeting a lot of new people at once. It's kind of like the first day at a new school! And it can be completely overwhelming for a nervous animal. Preparation is priceless in this scenario, not only for your new pet, but also for you and the rest of the family.

TIPS FOR SHARING YOUR HOME

If you're getting a dog, add a comfy bed in several rooms. Your pet will feel more comfortable knowing that it has its own spaces to relax, as it may take your pet a while to figure out which parts of the house it wants to spend most of its time in. Do you have vertical blinds, pooling drapes, or long curtain cords that could become strangulation hazards for an animal? Get down on your hands and knees and consider your home from the point of view of your new cat, dog, or house bunny! Try to identify dangerous objects and remove them or move them to higher ground.

You might want to roll up and store any special rugs you have until your new pet is fully house trained. You might want to cover your nice couch with an old blanket you don't care about getting hair on. If you or a family member get stressed because an expensive piece of furniture gets dirtied or damaged by your pet, your animal companion is going to feel that stress reflected back at it. It just arrived, and it's trying its best! And it doesn't have any concept of how much your parents spent on home decor, so try to avoid this becoming a problem before it starts.

Is your home safe? Get down on the floor and explore it from your pet's point of view. While you're down there, you may be tempted to relax and stay for a while!

Likewise, if you make sure your pet has plenty of toys it is allowed to play with, it will be much less likely to gnaw on your things! Make sure that any plants in and around your home are not poisonous to pets. When your new animal companion arrives, it is going to be so curious to check out its new home! The last thing you want is for it to discover that a plant is poisonous before you do.

YOUR NEW ROOMMATE

It is best if you can bring your new pet home at the beginning of a weekend or at some other time when you can clear your schedule and make plenty of time to hang out together. This way, you and your new pet can spend a few solid days in close proximity, adjusting to both of your new circumstances.

As soon as your pet arrives at home, you will probably want to implement some kind of training for it. Those first few days when your pet is getting its bearings are really important in terms of how it will continue to navigate its new space. For the sake of consistency, you should set up some house rules and expectations ahead of time that all of your existing family members can agree on. For example, will your pet be allowed to sit on the sofa? Will you let your dog sleep in your bed with you? Will you let it go under the covers if it wants to? Will you let your cat walk on the kitchen table? It's not fair, when you're training your pet, to let it do certain things sometimes and then at other times to tell it no. This would create confusion for any kind of animal,

Scratching comes naturally to cats and while you can't stop them from doing it, you can give them a scratching post to work on instead of the couch.

including humans! Give your pet every opportunity to successfully follow house rules by consistently enforcing the ones you and your family have decided on, and go slowly at first with introducing new people to your pet. It is best to give your pet a couple of weeks to get used to its new life before you start inviting visitors over to meet it. Show your friends some cute photos for now and tell them they can come over when your pet is ready! Those first few days are going to fly by, and before you know it, you'll be catering to your pet's daily needs as part of your regular routine.

PROFESSIONAL HELP

The shelter you adopt from should be able to give you advice about a local veterinarian with specialist knowledge in the species of animal you have taken home. Remember that the more unusual your type of pet, the more difficult it may be to find someone who really knows a lot about its needs. It is your responsibility to learn as much as you can about your pet and to find it the care that it deserves. Just as you are beginning a new and hopefully long-lasting relationship with your animal, you are also beginning a new and hopefully long-lasting relationship with your vet! So choose one wisely.

This whole joyful period after your pet joins your family is going to be a tremendous learning experience for you, your family, and your new animal companion. It may take a few days for it to get settled into its new home, or it may take a few weeks. One of the most important things for you to exercise is your patience. While you can do all of the research possible on the type of pet you have brought home, you need to remember that ultimately this animal is an individual, just like you are. Be consistent and be kind, and the relationship you build together is sure to have solid foundations with room for both of you to grow together. Enjoy this time of extreme change and be grateful for the opportunity. You are embarking on one of the most profound relationships of your life. You are now responsible for another living creature!

Veterinarians are among the most well-respected professionals in America. It takes around ten years of education and training to become a practicing vet.

Whichever kind of pet you have brought home, you will want to schedule an appointment with a veterinarian pretty soon after its arrival. As long as you have adopted your pet from a responsible source, you should be given some advice regarding when and where to go. Remember your veterinarian is likely to be very busy, and your appointment will quickly be over, so it's important to go prepared. The vet might have a checklist of information he or she needs to give you, but he or she won't know how much research you have already done. To make the most of your time, be sure to arrive armed with a list of questions you want answered!

10 GREAT QUESTIONS TO ASK YOUR VETERINARIAN

1. What is considered a healthy amount of exercise for my pet?

2. What kind of grooming does my pet need and how often?

3. Is my pet at a healthy weight?

4. How can I make sure that my pet doesn't get lonely?

5. Can I share some of my dinner with my pet, or should it only eat its own food?

6. How much water does my pet need to drink?

7. Does my pet need any vaccinations?

8. Can I travel with my pet?

9. Does my pet need any dental attention?

10. Is it fair to project my pet's image and personality on social media?

Chapter Five

DAILY LIFE TOGETHER

Those first few weeks are going to pass by very quickly. If all goes well, before you know it, your new pet will become a full-fledged member of your family, and you will slip into a steady routine of caring for one another. One of the first things you're going to need to figure out, in order to reach that point, is a diet that works for your pet. This is something that may take some work and require some room for trial and error, but at the heart of this task, you will find yourself with another opportunity to be ethically consistent with the philosophy of animal rights.

WHAT'S ON THE MENU?

When it comes to our pets' dietary needs, it is common for humans not to put a lot of thought into options and to feed their pets the same drab food for every meal, which is strange when we consider how much time we spend thinking about our own meals and nutrition. Additionally, commercial pet foods have existed only

Think about the ingredients in your pet's food. It takes only a moment to read the packaging and compare different products.

since the previous century. It's not like animals have always eaten prepackaged meals; it's just that the big pet food manufacturers have made it very cheap and convenient for people to buy their products, and these days, people lead busy lives. It's easy to assume that since they're everywhere, those products must be the only option.

COMMERCIAL PRODUCTS

Most of us know that commercial pet foods are available in supermarkets, with different-colored packaging and photos of cute animals on the wrappers, but we don't tend to know much about what goes into those products or if they are the most nutritious options available for our pets. Part of taking care of your animal companion ethically is exploring every avenue in terms of potentially improving your pet's health and happiness, as well as taking into consideration the impact that doing so has on other animals further along the food chain.

If you ask a lot of pet owners why they feed meat products to their animals, they might tell you that they do so because they think it's natural. But is it natural for dogs and cats to eat processed meat products often only designated to them once deemed unpalatable for human consumption? The meat that goes into most commercial pet foods is of the lowest grade imaginable. And more to the point, if people were really concerned with providing their pets with a "natural" diet, they would be feeding them whole birds or mice and allowing them to hunt for themselves in the wild. This idea of a natural diet simply doesn't apply to domesticated animals. It doesn't make any sense to use that excuse.

PLANT HEALTH

Besides, animals in the wild typically eat a lot of plant matter, too. And contrary to popular opinion, the nutritional needs of both dogs and cats can actually be met with a balanced vegan diet and some specific supplements. Of course, it is important to consult your veterinarian before changing your pet's diet. While dogs are omnivores and thus can adapt easily to a vegetarian diet, cats are obligate (or natural) carnivores and, as such, must be treated with care. With a little research, you will be able to find companies that produce both vegetarian and vegan pet foods, many of which do not test on animals in laboratories

Be sure to wash all vegetables before feeding them to your pet, just as you would for yourself. You don't want to expose your beloved pet to harmful pesticides.

(as some of the giants of the industry do). It is very important to consider where you're spending your money and what kind of industry you are supporting when debating this issue. It is easy to feel like you don't have a choice in what you feed your pet, but there are many options out there.

Some animals, like rabbits for example, should only be fed a vegetarian diet. In fact, around three-quarters of a rabbit's diet should be leafy greens, supplemented with other vegetables and fruits. You can have a lot of fun at your local market finding your rabbit's favorite foods. Will it prefer arugula, spinach, or watercress? Carrots, broccoli, or celery?

SHOULD I HAVE MY PET NEUTERED OR SPAYED?

The arguments for and against neutering or spaying an animal are complicated. It is very possible to see the points of view from both sides. At first glance, it does not seem like it could be ethical to remove an animal's ability to reproduce. In other countries, notably Sweden and Norway, neutering and spaying are extremely rare! Only a tiny percentage of pets there are altered, and it is usually done to ease behavioral problems. However, those countries are not dealing with an overpopulation crisis in animal shelters, such as in the United States.

The rise of neutering and spaying pets since the 1970s has dramatically reduced the numbers of unwanted animals euthanized each year. This system is effective and serving its purpose. Although we may feel uncomfortable with the idea of voluntarily taking our pet to the veterinarian for surgery, it is important to realize that most animals experience relatively little discomfort during the procedure. Anesthetics are used during surgery, and pain medication is typically given afterward. Pets can be back to normal within a couple of days.

According to the ASPCA, in addition to curbing the overpopulation crisis, there are also both medical and behavioral benefits for your pet. The ASPCA advocates neutering or spaying your animal, stating that it increases the chances of a longer and healthier life. Talk to your veterinarian about your options.

A BALANCED DIET

If you choose to make your own pet food, which is, happily, another very possible option, be sure to follow trustworthy recipes and monitor your pet closely to see if the food you have made agrees with it. Most dogs' and cats' health will improve on a vegetarian or vegan diet, but occasionally this might not be the case—so if this happens to your pet, use your common sense!

Whatever kind of animal your pet is, it's best if you can speak to your veterinarian before making any bold changes to its diet. Your vet should be able to give you helpful advice related to your pet's specific needs and give you tips for monitoring any changes to its weight, mood, or well-being. Our pets' relationship with food, just like ours, is integral

to their enjoyment and experience of life. Finding a diet that works for them is vital.

RESPONSIBLE RESEARCH

There are going to be a lot of decisions you will need to make regarding your pet, especially at first, for which you will want to consult your veterinarian. This might not always be possible and will not always be advisable. Veterinarians are highly trained, busy professionals, and as such are not there to answer to every whimsical query you can come up with, as fun as that could be. There is a vast landscape of information available to you in books,

WHAT ABOUT IF I GO ON VACATION?

Other people you might need to communicate with about your animal companion, at times, are pet sitters. You might sometimes be able to leave your pet with a family member or friend for a short time, if he or she is available and invested, but of course those people have their own busy lives, too. They can't drop everything just because you're going on vacation! Often it's more responsible to hire someone who actually wants to make time for your pet, and some quick research should locate a reliable pet-sitting service close to you. Depending on its temperament, your pet will most likely be more comfortable staying at home with a sitter, or even going to the sitter's house, than it would feel surrounded by unfamiliar animals in kennels. Be sure to have a checklist of information ready to tell the pet sitter when you meet him or her (which you should always do before you agree to hand over responsibility of your pet), and write it down, too, in case he or she needs to double-check something once you're gone.

If you're going to be traveling often, explore your options for bringing your pets along. They might be a little timid at first, but providing they trust you, many animals will enjoy a new adventure. Use your intuition.

Pet stores might not be the right place to find your new cat, but you should still be able to get a wide range of suitable accessories for him there, including carriers for long drives and plane rides.

documentaries, and online, which you should be able to harness to achieve a deeper understanding of your animal companion before you pick up the phone and call your vet. And most of the time, that should be enough.

This is another case for common sense, though. If your pet is sick or acting unusually, don't rely on untrustworthy websites and other nonspecific information to assess a medical emergency. Diagnosing your pet's health problems on the internet can be tempting but risky. You need a find a balance somewhere, and you don't want it to be at the expense of your pet.

When it comes to ethical pet ownership, there is a never-ending supply of questions to consider. Do your research, follow your instincts, and know that it's never too late to make positive changes to your pet's life. Keep an open mind, and always give your pet the companionship it deserves.

GLOSSARY

adoption A process by which a person voluntarily chooses to care for an animal in need.

breed (noun) A group of living creatures who share certain traits that are not shared with other members of the same species.

breed (verb) To produce offspring.

companion An animal with whom one shares his or her life.

consent Permission or agreement for something to happen.

domestication Taming of entire species of animals through generations of deliberate breeding.

ethical Concerning morals or the principles of morality.

euthanasia The act of painlessly ending a life in order to relieve pain and suffering.

exotic Introduced from somewhere distant, not native.

foster To take care of an animal for a limited time.

humane Marked by compassion or benevolence.

moral Relating to the principles of right and wrong.

neuter To castrate a male animal.

pet A domestic animal kept for companionship.

practical Manifested through action rather than ideas.

sentient Capable of perceiving or feeling things.

spay To sterilize a female animal.

species A group of living creatures consisting of similar individuals with the ability to exchange genes and interbreed.

theoretical Based on a calculated concept rather than practical experience.

veganism The practice of not eating or using any animal products.

vegetarianism The practice of not eating animals.

FOR MORE INFORMATION

American Society for the Prevention of Cruelty to Animals (ASPCA)
424 E 92nd Street
New York, NY 10128-6804
(212) 876-7700
Website: http://www.aspca.org
Facebook, Twitter, and Instagram: @ASPCA
The ASPCA is one of the largest humane societies in the world and was the first to be established in North America.

Animal Alliance of Canada (AAC)
#101-221 Broadview Avenue
Toronto, ON M4M 2G3
Canada
(416) 462-9541
Website: http://www.animalalliance.ca
Facebook: @AnimalAllianceofCanada
Twitter: @animal_alliance
Instagram: @animalalliance
The AAC is a nonprofit organization committed to the protection of all animals and to the promotion of a harmonious relationship between humans, animals, and the natural world.

Best Friends Animal Society
5001 Angel Canyon Road

Kanab, UT 84741-5000
(435) 644-2001
Website: http://www.bestfriends.org
Facebook and Twitter: @bestfriends
Best Friends Animal Society is the only nation-
al animal welfare organization focused exclu-
sively on ending the killing of dogs and cats in
America's shelters.

Canadian Federation of Humane Societies (CFHS)
30 Concourse Gate, 102
Ottawa, ON K2E 7V7
Canada
(613) 224-8072
Website: http://www.cfhs.ca
Facebook and Twitter: @CFHS
The CFHS is a charitable organization originally
founded in 1957 by individual humane societies
and Societies for the Prevention of Cruelty to Animals across Canada.

Defenders of Animal Rights
14412 Old York Road
PO Box 25
Phoenix, MD 21131
Website: http://www.adopt-a-pet.org
Facebook: @DefendersofAnimalRights
Defenders of Animal Rights is a nonprofit organization
founded in 1975 and dedicated to eliminating cru-
elty to all animals.

Humane Society International
1255 23rd Street NW, Suite 450
Washington, DC 20037
(202) 452-1100
Website: http://www.humanesociety.org
Facebook, Twitter, and Instagram: @HumaneSociety
Founded in 1954, the Humane Society of the
    United States is the nation's largest animal
    protection organization.

People for the Ethical Treatment of Animals (PETA)
501 Front Street
Norfolk, VA 23510
(757) 622-7382
Website: http://www.peta.org
Facebook, Twitter, and Instagram: @peta
PETA is the largest animal rights organization in
    the world, with more than 6.5 million members
    and supporters.

FOR FURTHER READING

Bekoff, Mark, and Jessica Pierce. *The Animals' Agenda: Freedom, Compassion, and Coexistence in the Human Age.* Boston, MA: Beacon, 2017.

De Waal, Frans. *Are We Smart Enough to Know How Smart Animals Are?* New York, NY: Norton, 2017.

Filardi, Christine. *Home Cooking for Your Dog: 75 Holistic Recipes for a Healthier Dog.* New York, NY: Abrams, 2013.

Griffin, Paul. *Stay with Me.* London, UK: Speak, 2012.

Hurn, Samantha. *Humans and Other Animals: Cross-Cultural Perspective on Human-Animal Interactions.* London, UK: Pluto, 2012.

Monninger, Joseph. *Whippoorwill.* Boston, MA: HMH for Young Readers, 2015.

Morrell, Virginia. *How We Know Animals Think and Feel.* New York, NY: Broadway, 2014.

Northrop, Michael. *Rotten.* New York, NY: Scholastic, 2013.

Pierce, Jessica. *Run Spot, Run: The Ethics of Keeping Pets.* Chicago, IL: University of Chicago Press, 2016.

Woodford, Rick. *Feed Your Best Friend Better.* Kansas City, MO: Andrew McMeel, 2012.

BIBLIOGRAPHY

American Humane. "Animal Shelter Euthanasia." August 25, 2016. https://www.americanhumane.org/fact-sheet/animal-shelter-euthanasia-2.

Becker, Karen. "What You Need to Know Before Bringing Home a New Pet." Healthy Pets, October 26, 2010. https://healthypets.mercola.com/sites/healthypets/archive/2010/10/26/preparing-household-for-a-new-pet-dog-or-pet-cat.aspx.

Bjorkenstam, Melissa. "Legal Rights for Animals." Petfinder. Retrieved December 16, 2017. https://www.petfinder.com/helping-pets/information-on-helping-pets/legal-rights-animals.

Carroll, Vivian. "When Should You Take Your New Puppy to the Vet?" PetMD, May 18, 2011. http://www.petmd.com/blogs/purelypuppy/2011/may/when_should_you_take_your_new_puppy_to_the_vet-11184.

Cotter, Mary E. "9 Common Rabbit Myths." Petfinder. Retrieved December 16, 2017. https://www.petfinder.com/pet-care/rabbit-care/common-rabbit-myths.

Crawford, Amy. "Is It Ethical to Keep Pets?" *Boston Globe*, May 15, 2016. https://www.bostonglobe.com/ideas/2016/05/14/ethical-keep-pets/nB3VciaZzJKWUqOlmJVZ2J/story.html.

Davis, Susan, and Margo De Mello. *Stories Rabbits Tell: A Natural and Cultural History of a Misunderstood Creature.* Herndon, VA: Lantern, 2003.

Finlay, Kate. "Why Your Dog Needs Mental Stimulation." I Heart Dogs, July 21, 2016. https://iheartdogs.com /why-your-dog-needs-mental-stimulation.

Herzog, Hal. "The Decision to Neuter Pets Just Got More Complicated." Huffington Post, March 1, 2013. https://www.huffingtonpost.com/hal-herzog/the-ethics -of-neutering_b_2790315.html.

Jackson, Jo. "Where Do Dogs from Pet Stores Come From?" Daily Puppy, February 20, 2014. http:// dogcare.dailypuppy.com/dogs-pet-stores-come-from -7593.html.

Korneliussen, Ida. "Should Dogs Be Neutered?" ScienceNordic, December 29, 2011. http:// sciencenordic.com/should-dogs-be-neutered.

Lin, Doris. "Is Pet Ownership Ethical?" ThoughtCo, July 16, 2017. https://www.thoughtco.com/arguments-for -and-against-keeping-pets-127752.

McRobbie, Linda Rodriguez. "Should We Stop Keeping Pets? Why More and More Ethicists Say Yes." *Guardian*, August 1, 2017. https://www.theguardian .com/lifeandstyle/2017/aug/01/should-we-stop -keeping-pets-why-more-and-more-ethicists-say-yes.

Pierce, Jenn. "Quebec Says Animals Are 'Sentient Beings' in New Protection Legislation." *Ottawa Citizen*, December 5, 2015. http://ottawacitizen.com /news/politics/quebec-says-animals-are-sentient -beings-in-new-protection-legislation.

Safran-Foer, Jonathan. *Eating Animals.* New York, NY: Little, Brown, 2009.

St. John, Allen. "Where *Not* to Buy a Dog: The Pet Store Connection to the Business of Puppy Mills." *Forbes*, February 22, 2012. https://www.forbes.com/sites/allenstjohn/2012/02/22/where-not-to-buy-a-dog-the-pet-store-connection-to-the-business-of-puppy-mills/#504dac71d1c2.

INDEX

A

adoption, 25, 29–32
American Society for the Prevention of Cruelty to Animals (ASPCA), 23
animal mills, 27–28
animal rights, 14–15
animal shelters, 23, 26, 29, 31, 32

B

behavior problems, 17, 49
birds, 13, 17, 20, 46
breeders, 25, 26–28, 29

C

Canada, 14–15
cats, 10, 12, 13, 17, 20, 24, 32, 46
commercial pet food, 45, 46
communication, 9, 39
companionship, 8

D

Defenders of Animal Rights, 23
disease, 21, 28
dogs, 9, 10, 11, 13, 17, 20, 24, 28, 46
domestication, 9–12

E

Egypt, 12
emotional support, 8, 9, 10
euthanasia, 32
exercise, 8, 24, 42
exotic pets, 20–21
expenses, 16, 39

F

fish, 21
food and nutrition, 8, 43–50
foster care, 32

G

geese, 14
guard animals and protection, 8, 14

H

hamsters, 17
health care, 8, 29, 39, 41, 42, 49
herding, 13
home environments, 16–20, 34–38
Humane Society, 23
hunting, 13, 20, 46

L

legislation, 14–15
longevity and lifespans, 16, 24

M

microchipping, 29
mistreatment, 28

N

native species, 20
neutering and spaying, 29,
    48–49

O

online information, 51–52
overpopulation, 28, 32, 48–49

P

pet sitting, 23, 50–51
pet stores, 25, 27–28
predators, 20–22

R

rabbits, 24, 27, 28, 48
reptiles, 21

S

safety (for pets), 34, 36–37
sentient beings, 14–15
stimulation, 17

T

temperament, 19–20, 33
toys, 17, 24, 37
training, 36–37
travel, 16, 50–51

V

vegetarian diets, 46, 49
veterinarians, 39, 41, 42, 49, 50
volunteer work, 23

ABOUT THE AUTHOR

While working from home as a writer and editor in Berlin, Lucy Shaw decided to sign up with a pet-sitting company and started looking after other people's dogs and cats while they traveled. Always walking and caring for different pets, she came to appreciate the varying needs of every animal as an individual and learned how to provide a loving home for many animal companions in need. A vegetarian for all of her adult life, she can't imagine eating meat. She writes books, does embroidery, and loves Bongo, the fluffy white ten-year-old baby-dog.

PHOTO CREDITS